USING COPYRIGHTED VIDEOCASSETTES

IN CLASSROOMS AND LIBRARIES

by

Dr. Jerome K. Miller

Copyright Information Bulletin No. 1

Copying in excess of fair use
requires paying clearance fees to the:

Copyright Clearance Center (CCC)
21 Congress St., Salem, MA 01970

CCC: 0-914143-00-X/83 $00.00+$1.00

Published and distributed by

COPYRIGHT INFORMATION SERVICES

P.O. Box 2419, Station A

Champaign, IL 61820

Phone: 217-356-7590

Library of Congress Cataloging in Publication Data

Miller, Jerome K.
    Using copyrighted videocassettes in classrooms and
libraries.

    (Copyright information bulletin ; no. 1)
    Bibliography: p.
    Includes index.
    1. Video recordings--Fair use (Copyright)--United
States. I. Title. II. Series.
KF3030.4.M54 1984   346.7304'82   83-20904
ISBN 0-914143-00-X   347.306482

Disclaimer

The opinions contained herein

reflect the author's informed opinion,

but do not constitute legal advice.

For Mary Carol

Preface

Through my consulting practice, I receive many calls from educators and librarians who are concerned about the legality of using copyrighted videocassettes in classrooms or in library viewing rooms, carrels, or auditoriums. Many callers tell me they received a written warning from the Film Security Office of the Motion Picture Association of America (MPAA) and they wonder if it affects their educational or library services. The MPAA warning notice was distributed to schools, colleges, and libraries by film companies in an effort to stop illegal performances. The opening lines of the notice read:

WARNING

"FOR HOME USE ONLY" MEANS JUST THAT!

BY LAW, as well as by intent, the pre-recorded video cassettes and videodiscs available in stores throughout the United States are FOR HOME USE ONLY.(1)

The notice continues with a statement of the proprietors' exclusive right to regulate performances of videocassettes. Educators and librarians who receive the warning notice frequently express concern about a key statement in the notice:

> [P]erformances in "semipublic" places such as clubs, lodges, factories, summer camps, and schools are "public performances" subject to copyright control.(2)

Educators seeing "school" in the quotation fear it denies the right to perform videocassettes in classrooms, while librarians wonder if libraries also fall under the ban on performances in public or semipublic places. The answers to these questions aren't always simple——and some inquirers are sure to be displeased with my response. Nonetheless, I hope this book will be useful to its intended audience.

A few educators and librarians call me to inquire about the "Home-Use-Only" warning labels on videocassettes. They frequently wonder if the labels are binding on their institutions. There appears to be little doubt these warning labels are advisory only, and do not affect the purchaser's performance rights——as great or limited as they may be.

This book does not treat the duplication of copyrighted videocassettes, as that topic has been covered in my earlier works, and the works of others. The topic does not appear to require redefinition at present, although that situation could change at any time.

Introduction

Every discipline develops a unique vocabulary which aids the specialist but confounds the novice. The legal profession is a prime example of this linguistic phenomenon, so those wanting to understand copyright must grapple with its vocabulary. This book uses two common words with unique meanings in the copyright law:

To "display" a work means ... in the case of a motion picture or other audio-visual work, to show individual images nonsequentially.(1)

To "perform" a work means ... in the case of a motion picture or other audio-visual work, to show its images in any sequence or to make the sounds accompanying it audible.(2)

The terms videotape, videocassette, and videodisc have specific meanings, but for simplicity, this book uses videocassette as a generic term covering all of those words. Videocassette, videotape, and videodisc do not appear to have unique meanings in the law.

ACKNOWLEDGMENTS

Thanks are due to many who contributed to the preparation of this book. Robert Wedgeworth, Executive Director of the American Library Association, granted permission to quote from Newton N. Minow's letter about using videodiscs in libraries. Burton H. Hanft supplied copies of court documents and a written response to Mr. Minnow's comments. Stuart Snyder, of MGM/UA, and Joan Powell and Michael Garofalo, of the Los Angeles County Public Library, supplied information about the MGM/UA performance license. Walter C. Allen read the manuscript and offered helpful comments for its improvement. My thanks to each one for their generous assistance.

Finally, my sister, Mrs. T.H. Pepin, has been a constant source of encouragement in getting this book published, and in many other ways. This book is dedicated to her as a token of my appreciation.

Chapter 1:
Proprietors' Rights

Statutory copyright law was created 270 years ago to protect authors' rights. It has been revised many times since, but its purpose remains essentially unchanged. The Copyright Revision Act of 1976 implemented this purpose by giving authors substantial control over various uses of their creative works:

Sect. 106. Exclusive rights in copyrighted works

Subject to sections 107 through 118, the owner of copyright under this title has the exclusive rights to do and to authorize any of the following:

(1) to reproduce the copyrighted work in copies or phonorecords;

(2) to prepare derivative works based upon the copyrighted work;

(3) to distribute copies or phonorecords of the copyrighted work

to the public by sale or other transfer of ownership, or by rental,
lease, or lending;

(4) in the case of literary,
musical, dramatic, and choreographic
works, pantomimes, and motion pictures and other audiovisual works, to
perform the copyrighted work publicly; and

(5) in the case of literary,
musical, dramatic, and choreographic
works, pantomimes, and pictorial,
graphic, or sculptural works, including the individual images of a
motion picture or other audiovisual
work, to display the copyrighted work
publicly.(1)

The first right restricts printing and other
reproductions. The second right gives proprietors
control over derivative works, such as new edi-
tions of books, films based on books, and clothing
displaying cartoon characters.

The third right, the "right of first publication," gives proprietors the right to keep pro-
ducts off the market. However, once a work legit-
imately enters the market--through sale, lease, or
lending--the proprietors loose this right.

The fourth right enables proprietors to
maintain artistic control and secure income from
performances. The fifth right has a similar
effect on displays of copyrighted works.

The new law substantially revised the right to regulate performances and displays. It removed the for-profit-performance-in-public limitation in the old law and replaced it with the fourth and fifth subsections described above. Although the new law enhanced the proprietors' right to control performances and displays, the law authorized certain public performances and displays without permission or fees:

> Sect. 110. Limitations on exclusive rights: Exemptions of certain performances and displays

> Notwithstanding the provisions of section 106, the following are not infringements of copyright:

> . . . .

> (4) performance of a nondramatic literary or musical work otherwise than in a transmission to the public, without any purpose of direct or indirect commercial advantage and without payment of any fee or other compensation for the performance to any of its performances, promoters, or organizers, if--

> (A) there is no direct or indirect admission charge; or

> (B) the proceeds, after deducting the reasonable costs of producing the performance, are used exclusively for educa-

> tional, religious, or charitable
> purposes and not for private
> financial gain....(2)

This is the legal basis for most free performances, such as storytelling in libraries and open-air performances by municipal bands. It also authorizes benefit performances at which performers and organizers contribute their services and the income after expenses is contributed to a nonprofit organization.

Although, Section 110(4) authorizes a broad range of users' rights, it imposes three key limitations in: "nondramatic," "literary [works]," and "musical works." Musical, dramatic, and nondramatic are not defined in the law, but they are clear enough without further comment. The restriction on performing videocassettes appears in the innocuous phrase, "literary work," as it is defined in the law:

> "Literary works" are works, other than audiovisual works, expressed in words, numbers, or other verbal or numerical symbols or indicia, regardless of the nature of the material objects, such as books, periodicals, manuscripts, phonorecords, films, tapes, disks, or cards, in which they are embodied.(3)

The limitation is in the first eight words: "literary works are works, other than audiovisual works ...." Because of this clause, free and benefit performances are limited to nondramatic literary or musical works—and audiovisual works are specifically excluded from this category—so they are excluded from the benefits of Section 110(4). Some audiovisual works might be regarded as musical works (a novel interpretation), but that offers little encouragement, as phonograph records and audiotapes are in a separate category, called phonorecords. Should anyone doubt videocassettes are audiovisual works, that term also is defined in the copyright law:

> "Audiovisual works" are works that consist of a series of related images which are intrinsically intended to be shown by the use of machines or devices such as projectors, viewers, or electronic equipment, together with accompanying sounds, if any, regardless of the nature of the material objects, such as films or tapes, in which the works are embodied.(4)

It appears, then, the Copyright Revision Act of 1976 intentionally or accidentally prohibits performances of audiovisual works, except under the educational exemption, the home-use exemption, or with the the proprietor's permission.

IS THE MPAA WARNING NOTICE ACCURATE?

Educators and librarians frequently ask if the MPAA warning notice is accurate. It is accurate insofar as it describes proprietors' rights and home-use rights, but it is seriously flawed because it:

A. uses without explanation a widely misun-
    derstood quotation from Section 106 of
    the House and Senate Reports, and

B. lacks information about educators' rights
    under Section 110(1).

The widely misunderstood quotation appears
in the third paragraph:

> The U.S. Copyright Act grants to the
> copyright owner the <u>exclusive</u> right, among
> others, "to perform the copyrighted work
> publicly." (United States Code, Title 17,
> Sections 101 and 106.) Even "performances
> in 'semipublic' places such as clubs,
> lodges, factories, summer camps, and
> schools are 'public performances' subject
> to copyright control." (Senate Report No.
> 94-473, page 60; House Report No. 94-1476,
> page 64).(5)

Questions center on the second quotation,
which is accurately copied from the congressional
reports accompanying the copyright act. Those
parts of the reports were clearly not intended to
prohibit performances in face-to-face teaching,
but to describe a new feature in Section 106
enabling copyright proprietors to control performances. The 1909 copyright act gave proprietors
little control over nonprofit performances of
nondramatic works, so public radio and television
stations and nonprofit clubs and societies used
nondramatic works without paying fees or obtaining
permission. The new copyright act reduced the
nonprofit loophole, without completely closing it,
so authors, composers, filmmakers, and others

could regulate performances of their works. The confusing quotation, above, is part of a long description of the proposed right to regulate public and semipublic performances. That part of the report is given here in its entirety, with highlighting for the portion quoted in the MPAA warning notice:

>   Under clause (1) of the definition of "publicly" in section 101, a performance or display is "public" if it takes place "at a place open to the public or at any place where a substantial number of persons outside of a normal circle of a family and its social acquaintances is gathered." One of the principal purposes of the definition was to make clear that, contrary to the decision in <u>Metro-Goldwyn-Mayer Distributing Corp.</u> v. <u>Wyatt</u>, 21 C.O. Bull. 203 (D. Md. 1932), **performances in "semipublic" places such as clubs, lodges, factories, summer camps, and schools are "public performances" subject to copyright control.** The term "a family" in this context would include an individual living alone, so that a gathering confined to the individual's social acquaintances would normally be be regarded as private. Routine meetings of businesses and governmental personnel would be excluded because they do not represent the gathering of a "substantial number of persons."(6)

When read in context, it is evident this confusing quotation was not intended to undermine educators' rights, but to describe the proprietors' new rights to control performances. The question then arises--if the statement was not designed to deny educators' rights to performances in face-to-face teaching, why are schools mentioned here? The sentence appears to have originated in the <u>Supplementary Report of the Register of Copyrights on the General Revision of the U.S. Copyright Law: 1965 Revision Bill</u>(7) and was repeated in subsequent reports. The Register's report provides ample evidence the Register and congressional leaders agreed the copyright act should include new provisions giving copyright proprietors broad rights to control performances and displays. The report also indicates a decision by the Register and congressional leaders to exempt performances and displays in face-to-face teaching.(8) Both points were well established by the mid-1960s, and the language ib the two sections of the bill and the reports was little changed in the twelve years remaining till the act passed in 1976.

There may to be several reasons "schools" appeared in Section 106 of the congressional and Copyright Office reports. First, the Register's comments on the teaching exemption express a concern the exemption might be misused for entertainment or cultural events held at schools.(9) Since the copyright bill contained a substantial change in the proprietors' control over nonprofit performances, it probably seemed important to indicate performances and displays in schools could fall within the proprietors' right to regulate performances and displays. It is unfortunate the Register did not include a qualifying phrase at that point in the report referring to exempt performances in face-to-face teaching.

A second possible cause for this apparent conflict is the fact that various sections of the bills and reports sometimes appear to exist independently of each other so statements in Section A may not reflect statements in Section Z. This can be seen in the confusion over educational broadcasters rights in Section 110(2) and the right to make ephemeral recordings in Section 112. (Some educators read Section 112 in isolation and assume they can copy sound recordings for class use.)

Speculation about the reason for including "school" in the quotation is incidental to the key point—which is more important, the law or the congressional reports? Congressional reports accompanying bills (often called legislative history) are significant explanations of legislative intent. They are frequently cited to clarify difficult or confusing points, but they do not have the force of law, so they cannot overturn conflicting statements in the law. Accordingly, when the law and legislative reports are in conflict, the law is supreme. Accordingly, the confusing quotation in the MPAA warning notice does not change the law authorizing performances of copyrighted videocassettes in classrooms.

I discussed this conflict between Section 110(1) and the reference to schools in the MPAA warning with Burton H. Hanft, MPAA's copyright attorney. Mr. Hanft assures me MPAA recognizes educators' rights under Section 110(1), so long as the conditions of that subsection are met. I asked Mr. Hanft for a statement to that effect which he graciously supplied. It appears in Appendix B, as part of a larger discussion of educator's and librarians' rights.

Chapter 2:
Home-Use Rights

Section 106 identifies the proprietor's rights to control performances but it also limits those rights:

Sect. 106. Exclusive rights in copy-
    righted works

Subject to Sections 107 through 118, the owner of copyright under this title has the exclusive rights to do and to authorize any of the following:

. . . .

(4) In the case of literary, musical, dramatic, and choreographic works, pantomimes, and motion pic-tures and other audiovisual works, to perform the copyrighted work pub-licly; . . . .(1)

This gives proprietors substantial control over performances, but it is limited by the last word, "publicly," which is defined in the law:

> To perform or display it at a
> place open to the public or at any
> place where a substantial number of
> persons outside of a normal circle
> of a family and its social acquain-
> tances is gathered; . . . .(2)

This authorizes performances in the home viewed by the family and its friends, and non-public perfor- mances elsewhere which are limited to a small number of viewers. There is little doubt the "publicly" limitation authorizes performances in homes, but its application to other performances is still unclear. The proprietors are attempting, with some success, to use this provision to restrict performances outside the home.

Chapter 3:
Educators' Rights

Educators' rights appear in section 110: "Limitations on Exclusive Rights: Exemption of Certain Performances and Displays." This section includes about ten exceptions to the proprietors' right to control performances and displays. Only one of these exemptions appears to apply to video-cassettes, and that is Section 110(1), which auth-orizes performances and displays in face-to-face teaching in nonprofit educational institutions.

Sect. 110.   Limitations on exclusive rights: Exemption of certain per-formances and displays

Notwithstanding the provisions of section 106, the following are not infringements of copyright:

(1) performance or display of a work by instructors or pupils in the course of face-to-face teaching activities of a nonprofit educational institution, in a classroom or simi-lar place devoted to instruction, unless, in the case of a motion pic-

ture or other audiovisual work, the
performance, or the display of individual images, is given by means of a
copy that was not lawfully made under
this title, and that the person responsible for the performance knew or
had reason to believe was not lawfully made; . . . .(1)

The house report defines several phrases
appearing in Section 110(1):

The teaching activities" exempted by
the clause encompass systematic instruction of a very wide variety of subjects,
but they do not include performances or
displays, whatever their cultural value or
intellectual appeal, that are given for
recreation or entertainment of any part of
their audience.(2)

"[I]n the course of face-to-face
teaching activities" is intended to
exclude broadcasting or other transmissions from an outside location into classrooms, whether radio or television and
whether open or closed circuit. However,
as long as the instructor and pupils are
in the same building or general area, the
exemption would extend to the use of
devices for amplifying or reproducing
sounds and for projecting visual
images.(3)

<u>Instructor or pupils</u>.-- ... the per-
formance or display must be "by instructors or pupils," thus ruling out performances by actors, singers, or instrumen-
talists brought in from outside the school
to put on a program. However, the term
"instructors" would be broad enough to
include guest lecturers if their instructional activities remain confined to
classroom situations. In general, the
term "pupils" refers to the enrolled members of a class.(4)

<u>Classroom or similar place</u>. -- the
teaching activities exempted by the clause
must take place "in a classroom or similar
place devoted to instruction." For example, performances in an auditorium or
stadium during a school assembly, gradua-
tion ceremony, class play, or sporting
event, where the audience is not confined
to the members of a particular class,
would fall outside the scope of clause (4)
of section 110. The "similar place"
referred to in clause (1) is a place which
is "devoted to instruction" in the same
way a classroom is; common examples would
include a studio, a workshop, a gymnasium,
a training field, a library, the stage of
an auditorium, or the auditorium itself,
if it is actually used as a classroom for
systematic instructional activities.(5)

To summarize, Section 110(1) authorizes a
wide variety of performances and displays in face-
to-face teaching, but it imposes some significant
limitations:

1. performances and displays of audiovisual works must be made from legitimate copies;

2. performances and displays must take place in a classroom or similar place devoted to instruction;

3. performances and displays must be part of a systematic course of instruction and not for entertainment, recreation or cultural value;

4. performances and displays must be given by the instructors or pupils;

5. performances and displays must be given in classrooms other places devoted to instruction and not transmitted by broadcast or cable television;

6. performances and displays must be part of the teaching activities of a nonprofit educational institution; and

7. attendance at performances and displays is limited to the instructor, pupils, and guest lecturers.

These seven provisions are simple enough to be readily applied to nonprofit schools, colleges, and universities.(6) In fact, they are so precise it seems unlikely they could be altered or limited by the MPAA warning notice or by warning labels on videocassettes. But the law is not always as simple as it appears, especially in the application of the sixth criterion, "nonprofit educational institution." The phrase is not defined in the law and it is becoming a source of confusion.

WHAT IS A NONPROFIT EDUCATIONAL INSTITUTION?

Questions remain about some applications of the phrase, "nonprofit educational institution," in Section 110(1). The phrase is not defined in the law, but the House Report explains:

> Nonprofit educational institution.-- Clause (1) makes clear that it applies only to the teaching activities "of a nonprofit educational institution," thus excluding from the exemption performances or displays in profit-making institutions such as dance studios, and language schools.(7)

To judge from the language of the law and the legislative history, it clearly authorizes performances in face-to-face teaching in nonprofit schools, colleges, and universities, but other applications remain unclear. The phrase also may authorize performances of videocassettes in classes offered by other nonprofit agencies, including health courses provided by hospitals, philosophy courses offered by religious organizations, genealogy courses offered by libraries, and remedial reading courses offered in prisons.

Aside from the nonprofit aspect described above, the phrase "educational institution" is not defined by the copyright act or its legislative history. It does not appear to have been tested in copyright court cases, but that and similar phrases have been applied in other cases. Some of the decisions appear to support the application of the Section 110(1) privileges to nonprofit institutions other than schools and colleges:

School for continuing education of businessmen was "educational institution" within meaning of Real Property Tax Law exemption.(8)

A free public library is an "educational institution."(9)

Nonprofit membership corporation which planned to conduct art classes for town residents and students in buildings on college campus, qualified as an "educational institution" within ordinance permitting educational institutions in a residential area when authorized by board of trustees of village, as corporation's objective had some educational value, it performed an educational function and it was organized exclusively for that purpose.(10)

But on the other hand:

Taxpayer, which espoused philosophy of cooperative education based on folk-school movement, which ran youth camps, a camp for families, one or two workshops and maintained a library containing 2,000 to 3,000 volumes, but which was not accredited, did not confer any degrees and offered no credits, was not an "educational institution" as such term was used in tax exemption statute.(11)

Ordinary meaning of "educational institution" which is exempt from inheritance taxes is a place where classes are conducted, such as schools and colleges, and not an institution which furnishes some education, no matter what branch, as incidental adjunct to its main purpose. (12)

Since "educational institution" does not appear to have achieved a uniform definition in the courts, another phrase in the house report deserves closer scrutiny. "Systematic instructional activities," is defined in the house report in its description of exempt performances in educational broadcasting:

The concept of "systematic instructional activities" is intended as the general equivalent of "curriculums" but it could be broader in a case such as that of an institution using systematic teaching methods not related to specific course work.(13)

That is not the clearest definition in legislative history, but it suggests a broad application to performance rights authorized in Section 110. Since the law and legislative history are not very helpful in defining educational institution, it may be useful to offer a preliminary checklist for those attempting to apply the Section 110(1) exemption to educational programs offered by hospitals, libraries, prisons, and other nonprofit agencies.

1. Do students receive frequent reading, field, or laboratory assignments, for which they are held accountable?

2. Do instructors assign grades based on papers, examinations, oral reports, and other reliable measures of pupil performance?

3. Are grades reported to parents, guardians, employers, or other responsible parties?

4. Are transcripts of students' grades available to other educational institutions?

5. Does the course lead to a recognized degree, diploma, license, or certificate?

Meeting these criteria does not guarantee nonprofit institutions they qualify for the Section 110(1) privileges. Conversely, because of the vagueness in the law, these institution may not need to meet the above tests to qualify. The issue deserves further attention.

EDUCATIONAL TRANSMISSIONS

Questions inevitably arise about the legality of transmitting videocassettes to classes through school- or institution-wide transmission systems. The copyright proprietors insist that privilege is reserved to them through Section 110(2).

Sect. 110. Limitations on exclusive rights: Exemption of certain performances and displays

Notwithstanding the provisions of section 106, the following are not infringements of copyright:

....

(2) performance of a nondramatic literary or musical work or display of a
work, by or in the course of a transmission, if--

(A) the performance or display
is a regular part of of the systematic instructional activities
of a governmental body or a nonprofit educational institution;
and

(B) the performance or display
is directly related and of material assistance to the teaching
content of the transmission;
....(14)

The key limitation appears in the first line:
"performance of a nondramatic literary or musical
work...." As noted on page 13, audiovisual works
are excluded by definition from "literary works,"
so they cannot be transmitted under the privileges
of Section 110(2). Suggestions are made that the
vague language in the house report, quoted on page
22, authorizes some in-building or campus-wide
videocassette transmissions. However, as noted
before, congressional reports do not supersede the
law, so it appears copyrighted videocassettes
cannot be transmitted to classrooms via closed-
circuit or educational broadcasts, except with the
permission of the copyright proprietor.

Chapter 4:
Librarians' Rights

The copyright act provides specific exemptions for performing videocassettes in homes, small groups, and in face-to-face teaching in nonprofit educational institutions, but a direct exemption was not provided for libraries or their patrons. If copyrighted videocassettes are performed in library carrels, viewing rooms, and auditoriums, the performances must take place under the non-public (home-use) or teaching exemptions, or with the the proprietors permission.

THE TEACHING EXEMPTION

The teaching exemption has obvious applications for school libraries or learning resource centers (hereafter libraries). Modern educational theories suggest classes should be divided periodically to provide specialized instruction for the pupils according to their needs. Classes are frequently divided so some pupils can review lessons they have not mastered while others study new material. Practical considerations frequently prompt teachers to send one group of students to the library for individual- or group-instruction while the other students remain with the teacher in the classroom.   As a result of these and other responsibilities, librarians or media specialists (hereafter librarians) are professional educators and serve as part of the teaching team.   Under these circumstances, a librarian who teachs a lesson or an entire course may perform relevant copyrighted works to support the lesson or course.

When applying Section 110(1) to instruction in libraries, the question frequently centers on the "place" requirement--the performance must take place "in a classroom or similar place devoted to instruction...."(1) The house report comments:

> The "similar place" referred to in clause (1) is a place which is "devoted to instruction" in the same way a classroom is; common examples would include a studio, a workshop, a gymnasium, a training field, a library, the stage of an auditorium , or the auditorium itself, if it is actually used as a classroom for systematic instructional activities.(2)

From this statement, it appears individual- or group-instruction conducted in the library of a nonprofit school, college, or university meets the "place" requirement.   But "place" is not the only requirement--as each performance must meet all the remaining conditions of Section 110(1), which are summarized on page 24.

One question remains about video performances in school and college libraries.   Some videocassettes purchased for class use, especially films purchased for film-study classes, will attract a certain amount of casual interest.   Since these materials probably cannot be performed for recreational purposes under the provisions of Section 110(1), these performances may be infringements which might be discouraged, unless permission has been obtained for this use or the use is authorized by a reversal of the Redd Horne decision, discussed below.

PUBLIC LIBRARY PERFORMANCES

Public libraries operate at a disadvantage in attempting to apply the Section 110(1) exemptions to classes they offer. If a public library is sued for performing videocassettes in classes it offers, it may have to prove:

1. it is a "nonprofit educational institution,"

2. the course meets the "systematic course of instruction," test, and

3. the library meets the other requirements of Section 110(1), summarized on page 24.

A lawsuit focusing on this issue could be a long and expensive and the outcome is not assured. A public library would appear to be at a significant disadvantage in such a case if an instructional performance was accessible to persons other than enrolled students.

I am not suggesting performances of videocassettes in classes offered in or by public libraries are illegal, but I would caution librarians to be careful to meet all the requirements of Section 110(1). (For another opinion see Burton H. Hanft's letter in Appendix B.)

DOES THE HOME-USE EXEMPTION APPLY TO LIBRARIES?

Librarians frequently wonder if individuals can use library video equipment to watch videocassettes. One might assume performances in viewing rooms or carrels occupied by one person, a family, or a small group of friends, meets the private showing requirement described in Chapter 2. Although the argument appears persuasive, it does not reflect a recent decision in <u>Columbia Pictures</u> v. <u>Redd Horne</u>, (The decision appears in Appendix D.) Redd Horne operated two video stores in Erie, Pa. equipped with many small viewing rooms. Each room contained seating for two to four persons and a color television receiver. Viewers chose a film, paid a rental fee, and saw the film on the television receiver. The videocassette playback machines were operated by an employee.

The plaintiffs charged the performances infringed their copyrights, as defined in sections 101 and 106. The defendant employed several avenues of defense, but its defense under copyright was based on the fact the occupants of each viewing room were single individuals, friends, or members of a family, so the showings were private showings as defined in Sections 101 and 106. The court found that since the performances were accessible seriatim to the general public, they were not exempt private showings. The court granted the plaintiffs' motion for summary judgement and, on October 13, 1983, awarded the plaintiffs $36,000 in damages. The parties were required to pay their own legal fees and the defendant was charged for court costs.(3) The decision has been appealed but the appeals court had not acted when this book went to press.

DOES THE REDD HORNE DECISION APPLY TO LIBRARIES?

The defendant was a commercial firm, so the decision does not appear to have direct application to nonprofit library performances. Furthermore, the case was heard in federal district court, and decisions at that level do not set precedent outside that jurisdiction. It would be convenient to cite these two points as grounds to ignore the decision, but it cannot be lightly dismissed, as every case sets a little precedent. This case leaves some unanswered questions and, unless it is overturned, it should prompt librarians to reconsider the practice of performing of videocassettes in carrels, viewing rooms, and auditoriums.

IF WE CAN SHOW FILMS, WHY CAN'T WE SHOW VIDEO?

Libraries have conducted film showings for over fifty years without question of copyright infringement, so it is understandable they should question this restriction on video performances. The change is a result of the Copyright Revision Act of 1976. Under the 1909 law, when the proprietors sold one print of a film, they lost the right to regulate performances of that title. To maintain control over performances, the film companies stopped selling theatrical films, and began distributing them through licensing agreements. Nontheatrical films, especially educational films, were sold to schools, colleges, and libraries under contractual agreements limiting exhibitions to free performances by nonprofit agencies. (Contracts and licenses are treated in the following chapter.) The new copyright act gave copyright proprietors a new set of rights to control performances of their films, but most firms retained the established system for distributing nontheatrical films. The old distribution procedures may have been retained for films, but videocassettes represented a new venture and the proprietors chose to conduct it under the more favorable rules of the new copyright act.

POTENTIAL SOLUTIONS

If the Redd Horne decision is upheld, it will sustain the proprietors' claim to control public performances of videocassettes, including performances in private viewing rooms viewed by individuals, families, and small groups of friends. In that event, the law probably will not authorize performances of videocassettes in libraries, except under the face-to-face teaching exemption. If the Redd Horne decision is sustained, librarians will face some difficult decisions in resolving their policies on performing videocassettes. Several solutions may be considered:

1. stop library video performances,

2. continue present practices and hope for the best,

3. limit showings to travelogues, inspirational works, etc., which can be performed under prevailing sales contracts,

4. obtain blanket clearances,

5. obtain performance licenses, or

6. amend the law to give libraries the right to free performances of copyrighted videocassettes.

The first alternative, terminating in-library performances, is unimaginative and should be discouraged. The second approach, maintaining status quo, is not recommended, though it may be the unofficial policy in many libraries.

The third alternative, using titles cleared for showing in the library, is safe, but it denies access to hundreds of other titles.

The fourth alternative, obtaining blanket clearances, is used by at least one large public library. It involves sending distributors a form letter advising that the library is uncertain whether it can legally show videocassettes in carrels, viewing rooms, and auditoriums. To avoid potential infringements, the library adopted a policy of limiting videocassette purchases to vendors who give the library written permission for free performances. (A sample letter appears in Appendix C.) Copyright proprietors have a longstanding and justifiable reluctance to grant indefinite, blanket permissions, so some vendors will forgo library orders before granting limited or indefinite blanket permissions.

The fifth alternative, obtaining video licenses, is new to libraries, but the procedure should be simple. MGM/UA recently sold its first public library video license to the Los Angeles County Public Library. The license consists of:

(a)   a one year lease for 18 feature films on videocassettes, and

(b) performance rights for the videocassettes in Los Angeles County Libraries, or patrons' homes or institutions.(4)

The sixth alternative, amending the copyright law, could be difficult, especially in the light of the Copyright Office's apparently unfavorable attitude toward libraries. If the Redd Horne dedision is sustained and an amendment appears to be the best solution to this problem, the amendment probably should consist of a new subsection (subsection 10) to Section 110:

Sect. 110.   Limitations on exclusive rights: Exemption of certain performances and displays

Notwithstanding the provisions of section 106, the following are not infringements of copyright:

. . . .

(10) performances and displays of motion pictures and other audiovisual works in libraries and archives qualifying under Title 17, <u>United States Code</u>, Section 108(a)(2), if:

(a) the performances and displays are open to the public at large;

(b) there is no direct or indirect admission charge; and

(c) The performance is without any purpose of direct or indirect commercial advantage.

Title 17, <u>U.S. Code</u>, Section 108(a)(2) identifies libraries and archives qualifying for the library photocopying privileges. Subsections (a)-(c) were adapted from other parts of Section 110.

The library community may not be able to get this amendment passed, but if it mounts a serious effort, the film industry may reassess performances in libraries, and begin offering reasonably-priced blanket permissions or licenses. These licenses or permissions can be included in sales contracts for videocassettes, or they can be sold separately.

CAN LIBRARIES LOAN VIDEOCASSETTES FOR HOME USE?

With the concern about infringing performances and the sale of performance licenses, readers may wonder if libraries can circulate videocassettes for home use. Fortunately, they can. Section 109(a) incorporates a common provision in modern copyright, which limits the proprietors' control over a work after it is published or enters commercial distribution:

Notwithstanding the provisions of section 106(3), the owner of a particular copy or phonorecord lawfully made under this title, or any person authorized by such owner, is entitled, without the authority of the copyright owner, to sell or otherwise dispose of the possession of that copy or phonorecord.(5)

The house report adds:

> Section 109(a) restates and confirms
> the principle that, where the copyright
> owner has transferred ownership of a par-
> ticular copy or phonorecord of a work, the
> person to whom the copy or phonorecord is
> transferred is entitled to dispose of it
> by sale, rental, or any other means. ....
>
> A library that has acquired ownership of a
> copy is entitled to lend it under any
> conditions it chooses to impose. ....(6)

This basic users' right appeared in the 1909
and 1976 copyright acts, but it may be amended
soon. The film industry is lobbying for an amendment requiring a surcharge on rentals of sound
recordings and videocassettes. The bills limit
the surcharge to commercial rentals, but librarians should be sure the noncommercial exemption is
retained when the bill passes. The House of Representatives Subcommitee on the Courts Civil Lib-
erties and Administration of Justice linked these
bills to the <u>Betamax</u> bill and they are expected to
pass together.

Chapter 5:
Copyright Contracts

When the film industry developed early in the twentieth century, the print-oriented copyright law offered inadequate protection for films. The industry responded by using contracts to supplement copyright protection for films. The practice began with theatrical films, but soon spread to the educational film market. Sales contracts permit purchasers to perform the films in classrooms and other approved locations, under specified conditions. Some contracts permit proprietors to seize the print if purchasers fail to observe certain contractual terms.

Many film librarians probably do not read the fine print in some of their contracts, as film libraries frequently violate certain contractual terms. One major firm previously included a clause forbidding rental or loan of the films to other institutions. It sold thousands of films to public library, school district, and university film libraries, knowing the libraries would loan or rent the films. The firm does not appear to have seized films for violating this contract condition, and it might not have the basis to enforce the clause, as it sold the films with the knowledge they would be rented or loaned. The fact remains, however, software contracts are usually written in the distributor's favor and must be treated carefully.

At the moment, the proprietors do not appear to be using sales contracts to prevent classroom or library performances, but that remains a viable option. Educators and librarians should examine the fine print in catalogs and on invoices to be certain the terms do not abridge their right to perform the titles they purchase. Readers who discover sales contracts which appear to restrict classroom or library performances are encouraged to send a copy to the author, in care of the publisher.

PERFORMANCE LICENSES

Performance licenses have been used by the film industry for over fifty years, but libraries are just beginning to acquire them. The only library video performance license known to be in force is one signed in 1983 by MGM/UA and the Los Angeles County Public Library.(1) I hoped to include the license in this book, but MGM/UA declined permission to reproduce it, as it is a preliminary document and the firm's standard video license was still in preparation and was not available when this book went to press.

The MGM/UA preliminary license contains key points which will probably be found in video performance licenses issued by many firms:

1. It has a specific duration.

2. It covers specific titles.

3. It authorizes in-library performances and the right to circulate the videocassettes for certain out-of-library performances.

4. The fee covers the lease of the videocassettes and the performance and loan rights.

5. Performances are to be non-commercial, non-theatrical, private, and non-paying. School and college use is limited to classroom performances.

6. The library may not edit, copy, broadcast, or transmit the movies.

7. The library may not advertise performances, except through in-house advertising.

8. The videocassettes must be returned to the licensor at the end of the contract year.

9. The licensor will replace defective videocassettes without charge, but damages caused by the licensee or its patrons will be repaired at the licensee's expense.

10. Penalty clauses are included in the event either party fails to fulfill its contractual obligations.

11. Traditional boilerplate is included to limit the parties liabilities and to guarantee fulfillment of the contract terms and effective communication between them.

It may be useful to discuss these items separately:

1. The MGM/UA preliminary license has a one year duration. The ideal license would have a multi-

year duration, or include an irrevokable renewal
option. Maintaining good public relations suggests this service should not be introduced if it
can cannot be continued on a similar basis for
several years.

2. The MGM/UA preliminary license identifies the
titles covered by the license, a necessary feature. Although librarians might like blanket contracts covering all the titles available from a
firm, few firms will accept such vague conditions.

3. The MGM/UA preliminary license includes the
right to in-house performances and the right to
circulate the videocassettes for home and institutional use. The in-house performance right is
the essential element here, but libraries already
have the right to circulate videocassettes for
home or institutional use under Section 109(a)
(described on pages 38-39), so they should not
undermine that right by purchasing circulation
rights as part of a performance license. Performance license will avoid the appearance of purchasing Section 109(a) rights by including the following statement, or something similar:

> The licensee's right under Title 17,
> U. S. Code, Section 109(a), to circulate
> copyrighted materials to library patrons
> is not subject to nor affected by this
> contract.

The law tends to reinforce custom, and if
library performance contracts routinely grant
rights libraries already posses, the rights may
eventually be undermined by the custom.

4.   The MGM/UA preliminary license includes the cost of leasing the videocassettes and the performance license.   This may become a common procedure, although some libraries will undoubtedly want to purchase the videocassettes independently of the performance license.

I   reviewed the MGM/UA license with a public library AV specialist who thought $150 per title for the performance right was too expensive for his multi-county, rural library system, but acceptable in a metropolitan area where the videocassettes would get heavier use.   His chief concern was leasing a videocassette for $29 a year when they usually sell for $55 and should last three or more years in normal use in his library system.

Unlike most library materials,   expensive audiovisual materials are frequently subject to price negotiation.   This should be especially true in negotiating performance licenses, as this is a new and unproven field, so vendors may be willing to experiment to find the best terms and prices. Clearly, a small library with five videocassette machines and two thousand cardholders should not pay the same fee as a large library with two hundred machines and thirty thousand cardholders.

5.   Prohibiting commercial and theatrical showings seems reasonable, as the licensor does not want free or inexpensive library performances competing with commercial performances.   The limit on private showings in the MGM/UA preliminary license is troublesome.   "Private" is not defined in the contract or the copyright law, but its opposite term, "publicly" is defined in the law to preclude library performances.   Contract limitations to "private" performances should rejected unless the term is satisfactorily defined in the contract.

The MGM/UA preliminary license is limited to "non-paying" performances. Many libraries charge small rental fees for borrowing or viewing video-cassettes. The MGM/UA preliminary license prohibits this practice and other video licenses may include this provision. Libraries that charge rental fees must stop charging the fee, or have it authorized in the contract.

The MGM/UA preliminary license also limits school and college performances to classrooms. The film companies know that performances at fraternity and sorority parties, PTA meetings, and other school and college events deprive them of a substantial income from their performance rights, so it is not surprising they will attempt to prevent libraries from collaborating with this common but illegal practice. This clause could create problems if an infringing performance is made from a videocassette borrowed from a library. Libraries should examine this restriction carefully to avoid undue limits on lending rights.

6. The ban on editing, copying, broadcasting, and transmitting videocassettes is to be expected, as those rights are sold separately.

7. The MGM/UA preliminary license prohibits advertising library performances in the news media, but permits advertising within the institution. This seems reasonable, since the film companies do not want low-budget library performances competing with theatrical performances. If a library wants additional advertising rights for its video performances, it may be able to negotiate a clause permitting certain low-level advertising in newspapers or on schedules or posters distributed outside the library.

8.   The MGM/UA preliminary license indicates the licensor will replace defective videocassettes, but videocassettes damaged by patrons or employees will be repaired or replaced at the lessee's expense. When I reviewed this clause with the public library AV specialist, he suggested the cost of repairing or replacing damaged videocassettes should be specified, as it could be very expensive.

9.   The MGM/UA preliminary license requires the licensee to return the videocassettes at the end of the contract term. A related penalty clauses states a failure to return the videocassettes for any reason whatsoever will result in a penalty of one thousand dollars per cassette. Library materials are sometimes lost or stolen, so libraries should attempt to modify the nonreturn penalty to exempt them from penalties for loss or theft by patrons.

The nonreturn provision also should allow time to recover overdue items, withdraw them from accession files, and ship them to the lessor.   A thirty—day grace period should be sufficient. Without a grace period, a library may need to begin withdrawing the videocassettes before the lease expires to avoid paying the penalty.

A library leasing multiple copies of some titles may want to include an early—return—for— credit provision, to obtain credit for low—use titles.

10.   Penalty clauses are a normal part of con— tracts. Libraries should require a balance in these provisions, to protect their own interests. Assurances by sales personnel that the company never invokes the penalties should be disregarded.

11.   Libraries   should seek a balance in the contractual boilerplate.   If the licensee must maintain a certain level of insurance or   notify the
licensor of an event via registered mail, similar
or balancing provisions should be included to
protect the licensee.

The MGM/UA preliminary license does   not
include a specific liability clause, though it may
be implied.   Libraries probably should require a
clause protecting the library from liability for
any illegal use of the videocassettes by patrons.

Unless the Redd Horne decision is overturned,
public libraries must make suitable arrangements
authorizing in-library performances of videocassettes.   This may include obtaining blanket permissions or an amendment to the copyright law, but
performance licenses appear to have the greatest
chance for success. Librarians who are not famil-
iar with this area probably should seek the assistance of an experienced copyright attorney or a
library copyright consultant to help the library
obtain the best possible terms and to avoid sur-
rendering their rights.

Chapter 6:
Are Warning Labels Binding?

About 1978, several major motion picture distributors began displaying warning labels on videocassettes. The text of the labels varies from firm-to-firm, but the following is typical:

Licensed only for non-commercial private exhibition in homes. Any public performance, other use, or copying is strictly prohibited. All rights under copyright reserved.

FBI WARNING

Federal law provides severe civil and criminal penalties for unauthorized reproduction, distribution, or exhibition or copyrighted motion pictures and video tapes (Title 17, United States Code, Sections 501 and 506). The Federal Bureau of Investigation investigates allegations of criminal copyright infringement, (Title 17, United States Code, Section 506).(1)

Educators wonder if the warning labels prevent them from using the videocassettes in classrooms, while librarians fear the labels prevent them from performing videocassettes in libraries.

USE IN LIBRARIES

In 1979, the American Library Association asked its attorney, Newton N. Minow (FCC chairman, 1961-63) to comment on using videodiscs labeled for home use only in public libraries. Minow's response raised doubts about the power of the home-use-only label to prevent libraries from loaning videodiscs for home use or performing them in private rooms in libraries. Although his comments address labels on videodiscs, they appear to apply to warning labels on all videorecordings:

> [I]ndividual use of the video discs in the library or at home would not constitute an infringement of the copyright owner's exclusive right to perform the work publicly. ....

> While there is thus little likelihood that a library's use of the video discs would constitute copyright infringement, it is possible that a copyright owner would attempt to prevent such use based on a contract theory. "For Home Use Only" could be read as simply a restatement of the copyright owner's exclusive performance rights as discussed above, or as a condition of the sale. If the video discs are sold to libraries by the manufacturer or his agent, it is unlikely that the legend could be held to be a condition of sale since library use would clearly be

contemplated by the parties. Furthermore, there is some case law which holds such restrictions invalid. In RCA Mfg. Co., Inc. v. Whiteman, 114 F.2d 86, 90 (2nd Cir. 1940), the court held that the legend on records, "Not Licensed for Radio Broadcast" constituted an invalid "servitude upon the records," analogous to resale price restrictions and other antitrust violations. See also, Universal Film Mfg. Co. v. Copperman, 218 Fed. 577 (2nd Cir. 1914) [condition on sale of film that it should not be sold or hired out outside of country where purchased held invalid.] In both these cases, the courts found restrictions on use inconsistent with the concept of an outright sale. If possession of the video discs was transferred by lease or license, such restrictions possibly would be appropriate and legally binding.(2)

Readers should treat his discussion of performances in private rooms cautiously, as they were written four years before the Redd Horne decision. I asked Burton H. Hanft, copyright attorney for the Motion Picture Association of America, to comment on Mr. Minow's letter:

You requested comments on the significance of the "for home use only" label which our clients affix to videocassettes and discs (herein called "cassettes") of their copyrighted motion pictures ....

The purposes of such labels is probably an attempt by our clients to inform
purchasers of a basic concept in copyright
law: that the transfer of title of a
cassette does not grant the purchaser any
right to perform the cassette publicly.
.... The label affixed to a cassette is
intended to correct that mistaken impression....(3)

The letter is as interesting for its omis-
sions as for its comments. Although Mr. Hanft
does not challenge Mr. Minow's statement that
labels are not binding, he does not advocate that
position either. One should not attach too much
significance to that, as it may have been prompted
by a perception the proprietors have a better
basis for regulating performances under Sections
101 and 106, especially as they were applied in
the Redd Horne decision. (The full text of the
letter appears in Appendix B.)

The question remains, do the labels limit
the use of videocassettes in libraries? Probably
not. Evidence has not been presented to suggest
the labels constitute binding contracts on purchasers, so libraries may be safe in that regard, but
that argument begs the central issue. Prescrip-
tive language on adhesive labels is one of several
approaches the proprietors use to protect their
right to control performances. But labels are
mere auxiliaries in this conflict. The proprietors' rights stem from Sections 106 and 101 and
they are the proprietors' main weapons for enforc-
ing their rights. Placing warning labels on
videocassettes and distributing the MPAA warning
notices provide evidence of the proprietors good

faith efforts to inform infringers of their errors. Ignorance of the law is not an acceptable defense, but a substantial lack of information about the seriousness of one's offenses may enable certain infringers to mitigate monetary damages, and the proprietors do not want that excuse to dull the sharp edge of the legal tools at their disposal. In short, the "label issue" is a side issue in the larger conflict over users' and pro-prietors' rights.

Librarians concern about the label issue is understandable, but its unfortunate this side issue deflected them from the central issue---the legitimacy of performing videocassettes in libra-ries. Let us hope future efforts focus on identi-fying the extent of copyright infringement in library performances and finding reasonable solu-tions.

USE IN FACE-TO-FACE TEACHING

The second aspect of this issue concerns the power of warning labels to deprive educators of their right to performances in face-to-face teaching. It seems unlikely the fine print on adhesive labels can undermine educators' precisely defined rights under Section 110(1). But, educa-tors should not be complacent as the fine print in purchase contracts can eliminate or restrict edu-cators' rights to classroom performances.

Notes

Preface

1. Motion Picture Association of America. Film Security Office. "Warning 'For Home Use Only' Means Just That." Hollywood, CA: the association, n.d., broadside. (Hereafter: MPAA Warning Notice.)
2. U.S. House of Representatives, <u>Report No. 94-1476</u>, Sect. 106. (Hereafter: House Report.)

Introduction

1. <u>United States Code</u>, Title 17, "Copyrights," Sect. 101. (Hereafter: Copyright Act.)
2. Ibid.

Chapter 1

1. Copyright Act, Sect. 106.
2. Ibid., Sect. 110.
3. Ibid., Sect. 101.
4. Ibid.
5. MPAA Warning Notice.
6. House Report, Sect. 106.

7. U.S. House of Representatives. <u>Copyright Law Revision</u>, <u>Part 6--Supplementary Report of the Register of Copyrights on the General Revision of the U.S. Copyright Law: 1965 Bill</u>. (Washington, D.C.: Government Printing Office, 1965), pp. 23-24.

8. Ibid. pp. 32-34.

Chapter 2

1. Copyright Act, Sect. 106.
2. Ibid., Sect. 101

Chapter 3

1. Copyright Act, Sect. 110.
2. House Report, Sect. 110.
3. Ibid.   4. Ibid.   5. Ibid.
6. For a thorough treatment of classroom use, see R.D. Billings, "Off-The-Air Videorecording, Face-To-face Teaching, and the 1976 Copyright Act," <u>Northern Kentucky Law Review</u>, Vol. 4, (1977), pp. 225-251.
7. House Report, Sect. 110.
8. <u>American Management Associations</u> v. <u>Assessor of Town of Madison</u>, 406 N.Y.S.2d 583, 585, 63A.D.2d 1102.
9. <u>Board of Directors of Fort Dodge Independent School Dist.</u> v. <u>Board of Sup'rs of Webster County</u>, 293 N.W.38, 40, 228 Iowa 544.
10. <u>Imbergamo</u> v. <u>Barclay</u>, 352 N.Y.S2d 337, 341, 77 Misc 2d 188.
11. <u>Circle Pines Center</u> v. <u>Orangevile Tp.</u>, 302 N.W.2d 917, 920 103 Mich.App. 593.
12. In re Goetz' Estate, 218 N.E.2d 483, 485, 8 Ohio Misc. 143.

13. House Report, Sect. 110.
14. Copyright Act, Sect. 110(2)(A).

Chapter 4

1. Copyright Act, Sect. 110(1)
2. House Report, Sect. 110.
3. Telephone call to the Clerk of the Court, November, 17, 1983.
4. MGM/UA Home Entertainment Group, Inc. "Public Performance Video License Agreement." Hereafter: MGM/UA License.
5. Copyright Act, Sect. 109(a).
6. House Report, Sect. 109.

Chapter 5

1. MGM/UA License.

Chapter 6

1. Label on Elephant Man, Paramount Home Video, 1980. [VHS videocassette]
2. Newton N. Minow to Robert Wedgeworth, April 23, 1979
3. Burton H. Hanft to Jerome K. Miller, August 12, 1983

APPENDIX   A:

THE MOTION PICTURE ASSOCIATION OF AMERICA

WARNING NOTICE

WARNING!

"For Home Use Only"   Means Just That!

By law, as well as by intent, the pre-recorded video cassettes and videodiscs available in stores throughout the United States are **for home use only**.

Sales of pre-recorded video cassettes and videodiscs **do not** confer any public performance rights upon the purchaser.

The U.S. Copyright Act grants to the copyright owner the **exclusive** right, among others, "to perform the copyrighted work publicly." (United States Code, Title 17, Sections 101 and 106.) Even "performances in 'semipublic' places such as clubs, lodges, factories, summer camps, and schools are 'public performances' subject to copyright control." (Senate Report No. 94-473, page 60; House Report No. 94-1476, page 64.)

Accordingly, without a separate license from the copyright owner, **it is a violation of Federal law** to exhibit pre-recorded video cassettes and videodiscs beyond the scope of the family and its social acquaintances—**regardless** of whether or not admission is charged. Ownership of a pre-recorded video cassette or videodisc **does not** constitute ownership of a copyright. (United States Code, Title 17, Section 202.)

———————————

Companies, organizations and individuals who wish to publicly exhibit copyrighted motion pictures and audiovisual works **must** secure licenses to do so. This requirement applies **equally** to profit-making organizations and nonprofit institutions such as hospitals, prisons and the like. Purchases of pre-recorded video cassettes and videodiscs **do not** change their legal obligations.

The copyright owner's right to publicly perform his work, or to license others to do so, is exclusive.

Any willful infringement of this right "for purposes of commercial advantage or private financial gain" is a Federal crime. The first offense is punishable by up to one year in jail or a $25,000 fine, or both; the second and each subsequent offense are punishable by up to two years in jail or a $50,000 fine, or both. In addition, even innocent or inadvertent infringers are subject to substantial civil penalties.

The companies listed below support the:

Film Security Office
Motion Picture Association of America, Inc.
6464 Sunset Boulevard, Suite 520
Hollywood, California 90028
(213) 464-3117

If **your** legal rights were violated **you** would insist upon seeking appropriate redress. So will the undersigned companies.

- Avco Embassy Pictures Corp.
- Columbia Pictures Industries, Inc.
- Columbia Pictures Home Entertainment
- Walt Disney Productions
- Walt Disney Home Video
- Filmways Pictures, Inc.
- Metro-Goldwyn-Mayer Film Co.
- Orion Pictures Company
- Paramount Pictures Corporation
- Paramount Home Video

- Twentieth Century-Fox Film Corporation
- Magnetic Video Corporation
- United Artists Corporation
- Universal Pictures, a division of
  Universal City Studios, Inc.
- MCA Videocassette Inc.
- MCA DiscoVision Inc.
- Warner Bros. Inc.
- Warner Home Video Inc.

APPENDIX   B:

A   LETTER   FROM   BURTON   H.   HANFT

LAW OFFICES
SARGOY, STEIN & HANFT
105 MADISON AVENUE
NEW YORK, N.Y. 10016
(212) 889-1420

BURTON H. HANFT
JEFFREY A. ROSEN
HARVEY SHAPIRO

EDWARD A. SARGOY
1902-1982
JOSEPH L. STEIN
1900-1981

August 12, 1983

Prof. Jerome K. Miller
2111 Galen Drive
Champaign, Illinois 61821

Dear Prof. Miller:

This is in response to your letter addressed to the Film
Security Office of the Motion Picture Association of America, Inc.,
which was referred to me for reply, and also subsequent correspondence
and conversations between you and me. Among other clients, this firm
has been retained by each member of the Motion Picture Association and
hence has an attorney/client relationship with such members in copyright
matters.

You requested comments on the significance of the "for home
use only" label which our clients affix to videocassettes and discs
(herein called "cassettes") of their copyrighted motion pictures with
respect to performances in classrooms, and also libraries which loan
cassettes to members of the public for performances in homes and also
provide video players in rooms in the library for performances of such
cassettes. This letter will express my opinion not only with respect to
such labels but also application of relevant sections of the Copyright
Act of 1976 to classroom and library performances mentioned above. My
discussion of library performances will also state areas of agreement and
disagreement with Newton N. Minow's letter of April 23, 1979 addressed
to the American Library Association.

The scope of this letter is limited to legitimate cassettes
which enter the market place by sale, or transfer of title. Cassettes
which reach libraries or schools through a series of license agreements
are outside the scope of this letter.

Although the language of each client's "for home use only"
label may vary, the differences are not significant. A typical label
affixed to a cassette container reads as follows:

> "This videocassette is for home use non-public
> exhibition in the United States of America and
> Canada only. Any other use is not authorized
> and is prohibited."

The purpose of such labels is probably an attempt by our clients
to inform purchasers of a basic concept in copyright law: that the

Prof. Jerome K. Miller
August 12, 1983
Page Two

transfer of title of a cassette does not grant the purchaser any right
to perform the cassette publicly. Although the purchaser of a cassette
may sell or otherwise dispose of it (17 U.S.C. §109[a], the purchase of
a cassette does not transfer to the owner other exclusive rights of the
copyright owner, including the right to perform it publicly (17 U.S.C.
§202). Many members of the public, including owners of camps, hotels,
factories, bars and restaurants, schools, libraries and government
entities, such as the armed forces and penal institutions, are under the
impression that the purchase of a cassette entitles them to perform it
in such places. The label affixed to a cassette is intended to correct
that mistaken impression. Whether the purchaser of a cassette who performs
it infringes the copyright owner's exclusive right to perform it publicly
is determined by the Copyright Act of 1976.

17 U.S.C. §110(1) sets forth the circumstances under which
performances in schools are not infringements of copyright. That section
reads as follows:

> "(1) performance or display of a work by instructors
> or pupils in the course of face-to-face teaching acti-
> vities of a nonprofit educational institution, in a
> classroom or similar place devoted to instruction,
> unless, in the case of a motion picture or other audio-
> visual work, the performance, or the display of
> individual images, is given by means of a copy that was
> not lawfully made under this title, and that the person
> responsible for the performance knew or had reason to
> believe was not lawfully made;"

Only performances in schools which satisfy each of the disjunctive clauses
of 17 U.S.C. §110(1) are not infringing performances.

We now turn to Mr. Minow's opinion that libraries which purchase
cassettes "for normal library circulation and in library use" may lawfully
do so provided libraries do not "exhibit the programs to a substantial
audience" or perform the cassettes "in programs for the public at large as
in projecting a movie on a big screen in a meeting room cultural center or
the like." I agree with Mr. Minow's opinion that libraries which circulate
cassettes for use at home do not infringe the Copyright Act; however, in my
opinion _any_ performance in a library infringes the copyright owner's exclusive right to perform the cassette publicly.

The words "perform" and "publicly", the two operative words of
the exclusive right "to perform the copyrighted work publicly" are defined
in 17 U.S.C. §101. It is unnecessary to quote or discuss the definition
of "perform" since there is no question that the exhibition of a cassette
in a library is a performance. The definition of "publicly" is:

> "(1) to perform or display it at a place open to
> the public or at any place where a substantial number
> of persons outside of a normal circle of a family and
> its social acquaintances is gathered; or
>   (2) to transmit or otherwise communicate a performance
> or display of the work to a place specified by clause (1) or
> to the public, by means of any device or process, whether the
> members of the public capable of receiving the performance or
> display receive it in the same place or in separate places
> and at the same time or at different times."

The first clause of the definition defines "publicly" in terms of places
at which the performance occurs. There are two such places: (a) at a
place open to the public, or (b) at any place where a substantial number
of persons outside of a normal circle of a family and its social acquaintances is gathered. If a place is open to the public, the number of
persons attending the performance is irrelevant. If a place is not open to
public, such as a club, factory, summer camp or prison, the composition and
size of the audience determines whether the work has been performed publicly.
Clearly, a library is open to the public even if a prerequisite to use the
library's facilities is a membership card, just as a theatre is open to the
public even if a prerequisite for entering the auditorium is the purchase of
a ticket. Thus, the fact that a library is open to the public mandates the
conclusion that any performance in a library infringes the exclusive right
of the copyright owner to perform his work publicly; regardless of the size
of the audience.

Mr. Minow does not focus upon the definition of "publicly" in
clause (1) in terms of "places" in the disjunctive. After quoting clause (1)
in his letter, he states "this clearly excludes home use, and we believe it
also excludes an individual's viewing of a video disc at the library because
the viewer typically would be in a private room and because a substantial
number of persons would not be gathered for purposes of viewing a program."
Thus, a basic fallacy in Mr. Minow's opinion is that he ignored the fact that
performances in a library occur "at a place open to the public". A room in a
library is not "private". However, let us assume arguendo that performances
in such rooms come within the definition of the second type of place, and an
insubstantial number of persons are present for each performance. In my
opinion such performances are infringing acts because the cumulative audience
which sees repeated performances of the same cassette becomes a substantial
number of persons.

Our firm recently supervised litigation on behalf of seven of
its clients in a fact situation remarkably similar to that described by
Mr. Minow, and the court granted a motion for summary judgment holding that
such performances "constitute public performance of the plaintiffs' copyrighted works and are therefore infringements of that exclusive right." The
case is cationed <u>Columbia Pictures Industries, Inc., et al. v. Redd Horne
Inc., et al.</u> and was brought in the United States District Court for the
Western District of Pennsylvania. A copy of the Opinion and Order, decided

Prof. Jerome K. Miller
August 12, 1983
Page Four

on July 28, 1983, is enclosed. The court granted injunctive relief and
will hold an evidentiary hearing on September 15, 1983 with respect to
damages, costs, expenses and attorneys' fees.

The defendants in the above case owned and operated two facilities
in Erie, Pennsylvania. At each facility defendants sold cassettes and
cassette players, rented cassettes for home use and also had approximately
40 booths with space for two, three, or four viewers, a television set
and an upholstered bench. The television set was wired to a cassette
player. Patrons paid a fee, selected a motion picture from a catalog,
entered the booth and closed the door. An employee of the facility started
the cassette player after inserting the cassette selected by the patron.

The sales of cassettes and players, and the rental of cassettes
for home use was not challenged. The complaint alleged that the unauthorized
performances in the booths infringed plaintiffs' copyrights. Plaintiffs
claimed that since the facilities were open to the public, all such performances were infringing acts. Plaintiffs also claimed that even if the
facilities fell within the definition of the second "place" in Clause (1)
of the definition, their copyrights were infringed because the cumulative
audience which viewed repeated performances of the same cassette comprised
a substantial number of persons. Finally, plaintiffs also claimed that
such performances were infringing acts because they fell within the definition of Clause (2) of the definition of "publicly" in 17 U.S.C. §101.

The defendants claimed that the booth was private; in fact a
living room away from home. This, coupled with the fact that only a
maximum of four viewers could view any performance at any one time, that
such viewers are either relatives or close social acquaintances and strangers
are not grouped in order to fill a particular room to capacity, necessitated
the conclusion that the performances were private. The booths in the
defendants' facilities are strikingly similar to the rooms in libraries
referred to in Mr. Minow's letter.

The court granted plaintiffs' summary judgment, holding:

> "We find that the composition of the audience at
> Maxwell's is of a public nature, and that showcasing
> the plaintiffs' copyrighted motion pictures results
> in repeated public performances which infringe the
> plaintiffs' copyrights ... We recognize that each
> performance at Maxwell's is limited in its potential
> audience size to a maximum of four viewers at any one
> time, however, we do not believe this limitation takes
> Maxwell's showcasing operation outside the ambit of the
> statutory definition of a public performance because
> the potential exists for a substantial portion of the
> public to attend such performances over a period of time."

Prof. Jerome K. Miller
August 12, 1983
Page Five

The court also held that the performances came within the second clause
of the statutory definition of "publicly" quoted above. It relied
largely "on a remarkably prescient discussion" of this portion of the
definition in 2 Nimmer on Copyright §8.14(C)(3) at 8-142. The court
stated that Prof. Nimmer concluded Congress intended "that if the same
copy ... of a given work is repeatedly played (i.e. 'performed') by
different members of the public, albeit at different times, this constitutes a 'public' performance." The court referred to an example cited
by Nimmer with respect to the peep show where, although no more than one
person at a time could observe a given performance, repeated playing of
the same copy of the material results in numerous performances seen by
the public. The court then quoted another example cited by Prof. Nimmer:

> "One may anticipate the possibility of theatres
> in which patrons occupy separate screening rooms, for
> greater privacy, and in order not to have to await a
> given hour for commencement of a given film. These
> too should obviously be regarded as public performances
> within the underlying rationale of the Copyright Act."

If the word "libraries" replaced "theatres", I believe Prof. Nimmer would
still reach the same conclusion.

For the reasons set forth above, it is my opinion that any unauthorized performances of copyrighted motion pictures in libraries infringe
the exclusive right of such copyright owners to perform their work publicly.

I would be pleased to discuss any questions or comments you may
have with respect to the substance of this letter.

Sincerely,

Burton H. Hanft

BHH:cr
Encl.

APPENDIX C

LETTER REQUESTING BLANKET PERMISSION

Library letterhead

Sales Manager
Video distributor
Address
City, state zip

Dear .... :

This library attempts to observe the copy-right law in the services it provides to its patrons. These services include showing copyrighted videocassettes distributed by your firm in library carrels, viewing rooms, and auditoriums. Questions have recently been raised about the legality of showing videocassettes in public libraries. All showings in this library are given free of charge.

Until this question is resolved, this library has adopted a policy of limiting its pur-chases of copyrighted videocassettes to titles supplied by firms which provide written permission to perform the videocassettes in the library.

Attached is a list of the videocassettes we now own which are distributed by your firm. Will you please send me a letter authorizing the non-profit library showings of these titles and other titles we purchase from you in the future

Sincerely, etc.

Enclosure

APPENDIX D

OPINION AND ORDER IN

COLUMBIA PICTURES V. REDD HORNE

IN THE UNITED STATES DISTRICT COURT

FOR THE WESTERN DISTRICT OF PENNSYLVANIA

COLUMBIA PICTURES INDUSTRIES,   )
INC., EMBASSY PICTURES, PARA-   )
MOUNT PICTURES CORPORATION,   )
TWENTIETH CENTURY-FOX FILM   )
CORPORATION, UNIVERSAL CITY   )
STUDIOS, INC., WALT DISNEY   )
PRODUCTIONS AND WARNER BROS.   )
INC.,   )
)
                    Plaintiffs   )
)
         v.   )   Civil Action
)   No. 83-0016 Erie
)
REDD HORNE INC., 2823 CORPORA-   )
TION, GLENN W. ZENY, Individu-   )
ally and d/b/a/ MAXWELL'S   )
VIDEO SHOWCASE, AND MAXWELL'S   )
VIDEO SHOWCASE EAST,   )
)
                    Defendants   )

O P I N I O N

INTRODUCTION

This is an action for copyright infringement brought under Title 17 of the United States Code, entitled "Copyrights," 17 U.S.C. Sects. 101-810 (1976). The plaintiffs, seven major motion picture producers and distributors, are either the owners or co-owners of copyrights in the motion pictures which are the subject matter of this lawsuit or are the exclusive licensees for distribution of these motion pictures or have by contract the right to enforce these copyrights.1/ The alleged infringement we are concerned with here results from the defendants' use of video cassette copies of these copyrighted motion pictures in a video showcasing operation. The defendants2/ operate retail outlets for home video equipment and accessories at two locations in Erie, Pennsylvania. These facilities, Maxwell's Video Showcase and Maxwell's Video Showcase East (collectively Maxwell's), sell and rent video cassette recorders and prerecorded video cassettes of copyrighted materials and also sell blank video cassettes. It is alleged that Maxwell's performs video cassettes of the plaintiffs' copyrighted motion pictures to customers at its facilities in violation of the plaintiff's exclusive rights under the federal copyright laws.

FACTS

The alleged performance of video cassettes at Maxwell's facilities is the sole basis for the plaintiffs' charge of copyright infringement in this particular lawsuit.3/ The plaintiffs base their claim of infringement on the argument that Maxwell's showcasing constitutes a "public performance" of the plaintiffs' copyrighted motion pictures, and is an infringement of the exclusive right to perform their copyrighted work publicly which is enjoyed by copyright owners. In order to place the discussion in the proper context, we find it necessary to set forth in some detail a description of the two Maxwell's facilities and the showcasing activities which allegedly result in infringement of the plaintiffs' copyrights before proceeding to an analysis of the applicable statutory provisions governing the issue.

The original Maxwell's Video Showcase opened on the West side of Erie on July 22, 1981. Maxwell's Video Showcase East opened some fifteen months later on October 29, 1982 following the success of the original Maxwell's and some area competitors. The west side store is approximately sixty feet wide by sixty feet long and consists of a small showroom area in the front of the store and the showcase area on the rear portion of the store. The showroom area contains the equipment and materials which Maxwell's has available for sale or rent and a counter area which is attended by employees of Maxwell's. This showroom area also contains dispensing machines for popcorn and carbonated beverages. There is a wall about three feet behind the counter area. The showcase area, or viewing rooms, are located beyond this wall. These viewing rooms are essentially private booths with spaces for either two, three or four viewers. The west side facility initially contained twenty one such rooms and was later expanded to contain forty-four viewing rooms. The design of a particular room may vary in shape from a square to a more triangular design and in size depending on the number of viewers it is designed to accommodate. The interior of the rooms does not vary significantly. A typical room is approximately four feet by six feet, is carpeted on the floor and walls, and is furnished with an upholstered bench at the back of the room and a nineteenth inch color television at the front. Maxwell's Video Showcase East is approximately twenty-four feet wide by one hundred twenty feet long, has a front showroom area similar to the one at Maxwell's Video Showcase and contains forty-one rooms of essentially the same design and interior decoration as the ones at the west side store. At both facilities approximately twenty percent of the rooms hold up to four people and the remaining will accommodate only two.

The procedure to be followed by a patron wishing to utilize one of the viewing rooms is exactly the same at both facilities. Maxwell's terms the use of these rooms an in-store rental. The rental is initiated by the viewer selecting the motion picture he wishes to see from a catalogue of the film titles available at Maxwell's This catalogue changes periodically within the addition of new titles to Maxwell's library of cassettes. The patron then reserves a room and is charge a fee for the use of the room and the video cassette copy of the chosen film if the cassette is available at that time.4/ The fee is based on the time of day and on the number of persons using the room.5/ The patron may then help themselves to popcorn and cold drinks before going to their assigned room. The cassette does not begin to run until the viewers have situated themselves in the room and closed the door. Closing the door to the viewing room activates an automatic signal in the counter area at the front of the store where an employee of Maxwell's starts the videocassette machine which contains the cassette selected by the viewer. The indiviual viewers may adjust the lighting in the rooms by use of a rheostat located in the room. They also may adjust the various volume, brightness and color levels on the television set, however, the video cassette machines are

all located in one central area on the wall behind
the counter in the front showroom and are operated
only employees of Maxwell's.

Access to a particular room is limited to
the two, three or four individuals who rent it as
a group.   Strangers are not grouped in order to
fill a particular room to capacity an no one can
enter a room which is occupied.   Maxwell's does
have a club for home rentals of video cassettes,
however, membership in the club is not a prerequisite for use of the in-store rental facilities and
at least a portion of Maxwell's in-store rentals
are the result of people waking in off the street
and requesting to view one of the cassettes.

Maxwell's has advertised on Erie radio stations and on the theater and restaurant pages of
the Erie Times newspaper.   There are also adverti-
sements resembling movie posters at the entrances
to the two Maxwell's facilities.

PROCEDURAL POSTURE

The plaintiffs filed the complaint initia-
ting the action on January 19, 1983.   The defendants filed an answer and counterclaim on February
28 and an amended answer and counterclaim on May
9.   The plaintiffs moved to dismiss the counterclaim on March 23 and briefs on that motion have
been submitted by both sides.   On May 31 the
defendants moved for summary judgment and the
plaintiffs countered with their own motion for
summary judgment on June 1.   Numerous briefs and
exhibits have been filed by both sides addressing
the issue before the Court for summary judgment.
The Court held a hearing on the motion to dismiss
and on the cross motion for summary judgment on
July 1.   The parties have stated, and the Court

finds, there are no issues of material fact which would preclude the entry of summary judgment in this action. We are, therefore, in a position to enter a ruling on all outstanding motions at this time.

DISCUSSION

A. Motions for summary judgment.

The plaintiffs do not contend that the video cassette copies of plaintiffs' copyrighted movies which are used in the defendants' in-store rental or showcasing, operation were obtained by any illegitimate means; and, in fact, the cassettes used by the defendants were obtained either by purchasing them from the plaintiffs or their authorized distributors. In other words, the plaintiffs do not allege that the defendants have no right to possess the particular video cassette copies they have purchased or that rental of such copies for in-home use infringes their copyrights. The complaint is based solely on the allegation that the defendants' showcasing operation is a public performance, as that term is defined by the federal copyright laws, and that the exclusive right to to perform a work publicly is retained by the copyright owner despite the sale of a particular copy of the owner's copyrighted work.

The proposition that a copyright owner may dispose of a copy of his work and at the same time retain all underlying copyrights which are not expressly or impliedly disposed of with that copy is beyond contention. Section 202 of the 1976 Copyright Act states that one may own a copy of another's copyrighted work yet not acquire any of the exclusive rights accompanying the copyright.

> Ownership of a copyright, or of any of the
> exclusive rights under a copyright, is
> distinct from ownership of any material
> object in which the work is embodied.
> Transfer of ownership of any material
> object, including the copy or phonorecord
> in which the work is first fixed, does not
> of itself convey any rights in the copy-
> righted work embodied in the object; nor,
> in the absence of an agreement, does
> transfer of ownership of a copyright or of
> any exclusive rights under a copyright
> convey property rights in any material
> object.

17 U.S.C. Sect. 202 (1976). The plaintiffs' sales
of video cassette copies of their copyrighted
motion pictures to the defendants resulted only in
a waiver of the exclusive distribution right held
in those particular copies sold, 17 U.S.C. Sect.
109(a) (1976), therefore, any other rights the
plaintiffs held in the motion pictures remain with
them in their capacity as copyright owners.

Those exclusive rights which are enjoyed by
the plaintiffs as copyright owners are enumerated
in section 106 of the 1976 Copyright Act, which
provides that, in the case of motion pictures:

> [s]subject to section 107 through 118, the
> owner of copyright under this title [17
> U.S.C. Sects. 101-810] has exclusive
> rights to do and to authorize any of the
> following:
>
>> (1) to reproduce the copyrighted work
>> or phonorecords;

(2) to prepare derivative works based upon the copyrighted work;

(3) to distribute copies or phono-records of the copyrighted work to the public by sale or other transfer of ownership, or by rental, lease, or lending;

(4) in the case . . . motion pictures and other audiovisual works, to per-form the copyrighted work publicly; and

(5) in the case of . . . the individual images of a motion picture or other audiovisual work, to display the copyrighted work publicly.

17 U.S.C. Sect. 106 (1976).

The rights granted by section 106 are sepa-rate and distinct and, as such, are severable from one another. The grant of one does not waive any of the other exclusive rights. See Interstate Hotel Co. v. Remick Music Corp., 157 F.2d 744 (8th Cir. 1946) (held that exercise of one of the exclusive rights granted under section 1 of the 1909 Act did not result in abandonment of the other of such rights). See generally 2 M. Nimmer, Nimmer on Copyright Sect. 8.01[A], at 8-11---8-12 (1983) (discussing the cumulative and severable nature of the exclusive rights granted by section 106 of the 1976 Act and citing Interstate Hotel Co., 157 F.2d 744, in support of the proposition). The plaintiffs' sales of videocassette copies of their copyrighted motion pictures which resulted in a waiver of their exclusive rights to distrib-ute those copies sold, 17 U.S.C. Sect. 109(a)

(1976), did not result in a waiver of any of the
other exclusive rights enumerated in section 106.
Thus the plaintiffs retain the exclusive right to
perform their motion pictures publicly despite the
sale of video cassette copies to the defendants.

"Anyone who violates any of the exclusive
rights of the copyright owner as provided by Sections 106 through 118 . . . is an infringer of the
copyright." 17 U.S.C. Sect. 501(a) (1976). The
issue is thus reduced to a determination of whether Maxwell's showcasing of copyrighted prerecorded video cassettes constitutes a public performance of the motion pictures embodied in those
cassettes. If it does it is an infringement of
the plaintiffs' copyrights.

The exclusive right of a copyright owner to
perform his copyrighted work in public is found
in clause (4) of section 106. We begin our analysis of section 106(4) with the definitions "perform" and "perform . . . a work 'publicly'" which
are found in 17 U.S.C. Sect. 101 (1976). "to
perform a work means . . . in the case of a motion
picture or other audiovisual work to show its
images in any sequence or to make the sounds
accompanying it audible." 17 U.S.C. Sect. 101
(1976). The House of Representatives report
accompanying the 1976 Act provides further explanation of what constitutes a performance of motion
pictures.

The definition of "perform" in relation to
a "motion picture or other audio visual
work" is "to show its images in any
sequence or to make the sounds accompanying it audible." The showing of por-
tions of a motion picture . . . must
therefore be sequential to constitute a

> "performance" rather than a "display", but no particular order need be maintained. The purely aural performance of a motion picture sound track, or of sound portions of an audiovisual work, would constitute a performance of the "motion picture or other audiovisual work"; but, where some of the sounds have been reproduced separately on phonorecords, a performance from the phonorecord would not constitute performance of the motion picture or audiovisual work.

H.R.Rep.No. 1476, 94th Cong., 2d Sess. 63-64, reprinted in 1976 U.S. Code Cong. & Ad. News 5659, 5677. There can be no doubt that the playing of a video cassette results in a sequential showing of its images and in making the sounds accompanying it audible. Video cassette showcasing, such as that done at Maxwell's, is a performance under the copyright laws. Our inquiry is thus further reduced to a determination of whether or not such performances are public and, therefore, an infringement of the plaintiffs' copyrights.

The applicable statutory definition states that:

> [t]o perform . . . it at a place open to the public or at any place where a substantial number of persons outside of a normal circle of a family and its social acquaintances is gathered . . .

17 U.S.C. Sect. 101 (1976). The plaintiffs contend that the definition found in clause (1) is written in the disjunctive form resulting in the creation of two separate categories of what is public, i.e., (1) at a place open to the public or

(2) at any place where a substantial number of persons outside of a normal circle of a family and its social acquaintances is gathered. The defendants argue that the definition consists of two complementary phrases designated to express congressional concern with the composition of the group viewing a performance as opposed to the place where the viewing occurs. In support of this argument the defendants cite the legislative history accompanying this portion of the definition of public performance

> Under clause (1) of the definition of "publicly" in section 101, a performance . . . is "public" if it takes place "at a place open to the public or at any place where a substantial number of persons outside of a normal circle of a family and its social acquaintances is gathered." One of the principal purposes of the definition was to make clear that, contrary to the decision in Metro-Goldwin-Mayer Distributing Corp. v. Wyatt, 21 C.O. Bull. 203 (D.Md. 1932), performances in "semi-public" places such as clubs, lodges, factories, summer camps, and schools are "public performances" subject to copyright control. The term "a family" in this context would include an individual living alone, so that a gathering confined to the individual's social acquaintances would normally be regarded as private. Routine meetings of businesses and governmental personnel would be excluded because they do not represent the gathering of a "substantial number of persons."

H.R.Rep.No. 1476, 94th Cong., 2d Sess. 64, reprinted in 1976 U.S. Code Cong. & Ad. News 5659,

5677-78. The parties' positions may create what amounts to a distinction without a difference; nevertheless, the language of the statute and its legislative history indicates that Congress' concern was with the composition of the audience. This conclusion does not emasculate the plaintiffs' contention that a public performance could occur in either a place open to the public in a general sense or in a place access to which is in some way restricted and which is therefore more in the nature of a semi-public place. <u>Learner v. Schectman</u>, 228 F.Supp. 354 (D.Minn. 1964), a case decided under the 1909 Act, holds that a performance may be found to be public even if the composition of the audience is restricted to some degree if, despite such restriction, a substantial portion of the public has the potential to attend the performance. <u>See also</u> 2 M. Nimmer, Sect. 8.14[C] [1], at 8--138-39. Maxwell's does not limit use of its viewing rooms in any manner other than a requirement that all viewers be either relatives or close social acquaintances. The defendants contend that this restriction in the use of the viewing rooms is enough to take Maxwell's showcasing outside the relm of a public performance. The plaintiffs argue that Maxwell's is clearly open to the public and that, at any rate, it is a place where a substantial number of persons "outside of a normal circle of a family and its social acquaintances is gathered."

We find that the composition of the audience at Maxwell's is of a public nature, and that showcasing the plaintiffs' copyrighted motion pictures results in repeated public performances which infringe the plaintiffs's copyrights. Our finding is based on the view that the viewing rooms at Maxwell's more closely resemble mini-movie theaters than living rooms away from home.

At least as regards the composition of the audien-
ces at Maxwell's, the showcasing operation is not
distinguishable in any significant manner from the
exhibition of films at a conventional movie theater.   Both types of facilities are open to all
member of the general public.   Access to the
actual viewing area of both theaters is limited to
paying customers.   Seating in both facilities is
of a finite number and, at both facilities, the
actual performance of the motion picture is hand-
led by employees of the theater.   We recognize
that each performance at Maxwell's is limited in
its potential audience size to a maximum of four
viewers at any one time, however, we do not
believe this limitation takes Maxwell's showcasing
operation outside the ambit of the statutory definition of a public performance because the potential exists for a substantial portion of the public to attend such performances over a period of
time.

Our conclusion that Maxwell's showcasing
constitutes infringing public performances is
bolstered by the second clause of the statutory
definition of public performance.   Under this
clause, to perform a work publicly means:

> (2) to transmit or otherwise communicate a
> performance . . . of the work to a place
> specified by clause (1) or to the public,
> by means of any device or process, whether
> the members of the public capable of
> receiving the performance . . . receive it
> in the same place or in separate places
> and at the same time or at different
> times.

17 U.S.C. Sect. 101 (1976).   Professor Nimmer, in
a remarkably prescient discussion of this portion

of the definition, concluded that Congress intended that "if the same copy . . . of a given work
is repeatedly played (i.e. 'performed') by different members of the public, albeit at different
times, this constitutes a 'public' performance." 2
M. Nimmer, Sect. 8.14[C][3], at 8-142. Nimmer
cites as one example the peep show where, although
no more than one person at a time can observe a
given performance, repeated plying of the same
copy of the material results in numerous performances seen by the public, Nimmer, foreseeing an
operation similar to Maxwell's, goes on to state
that:

> one may anticipate the possibility of
> theaters in which patrons occupy separate
> screening rooms, for greater privacy, and
> in order not to have to await a given hour
> for commencing of a give film. These too
> should obviously be regarded as public
> performances within the underlying ratio-
> nale of the Copyright Act.

Id. at 8-142. The two Maxwell's facilities each
have only one copy of a given film title and,
therefore, must perform the same copy of a given
work repeatedly. We find that Congress intended
that this portion of the definition also serve as
protection for copyright owners from infringing
performances such as those accomplished by Maxwell's showcasing.

B. Motion to dismiss defendants' counterclaim.

The defendants' counterclaim contains four
counts. Count one alleges that the sole motiva-
tion of the plaintiffs in bringing the infringement action which initiated this lawsuit was "to

drive the Defendants--Counterclaimants from the newly created showcasing market and to reserve that market solely to the Plaintiffs-Counterdefendants." Count two alleges that the activities of the plaintiffs "constitutes an unlawful tying arrangement in violation of the federal antitrust laws including the Sherman Act and the Clayton Act." We will address those two counts before moving on to the final two.

Groups with common interests may, without violating the antitrust laws, use the channels and procedure of the courts to protect their business and economic interests from interference by competitors. See California Motor Transport Co. v. Trucking Unlimited 404 U.S. 508 (1972); United Mine Workers v. Pennington, 381 U.S. 657 (1965); Eastern Railroad Presidents Conference v. Noerr Motor Freight, Inc., 365 U.S. 127 (1961). This exemption from the antitrust laws is limited by the requirement that utilization of the courts must be in good faith and not a mere sham. 365 U.S. at 144.

A good faith effort to enforce one's copyright is not conduct which violates the antitrust laws. Edward B. Marks Music Corp. v. Colorado Magnetics, Inc., 497 F.2d 285 (10th Cir. 1974); Alberto-Culver Company v. Andrea Dumon, Inc., 466 F.2d 705 (7th Cir. 1972). Our finding that Maxwell's showcasing results in an infringement of the plaintiffs' copyrights removes any suggestion that the infringement suit was a sham or brought in bad faith. Dismissal of the two antitrust claims is appropriate.

Count three of the counterclaim alleges, without elaboration, that the plaintiffs' filing of the infringement suit constitutes a malicious interference with the business relationships of the defendants. We are mindful of, and in agreement with, case law which cautions a trial court to construe pleadings liberally when ruling on a motion pursuant to Fed.R.Civ.P. 12(b)(6), however, even those decisions require no more than a consideration of all facts alleged and a drawing of all fairly deducible inferences from those facts. See Miller v. American Telephone and Telegraph Company, 507 F.2d 759 (3d Cir. 1974). Where, as here, no facts in support of the allegations are presented, dismissal of the claim is appropriate.

Count four is a claim for the breach of an implied contract of good faith and fair dealing. The facts in the record reveal no possible manner in which a claim based on an alleged breach of a contractual relationship between the plaintiffs and the defendants can be maintained. We will, therefore, dismiss the defendants' counterclaim in its entirety.

CONCLUSION

The defendants' showcasing operations at Maxwell's Video Showcase and Maxwell's Video Showcase East constitute public performances of the plaintiffs' copyrighted works and therefore infringements of that exclusive right. The plaintiffs' motion for summery judgment will be granted and, accordingly, the defendants' motion for summary judgment will be denied. The defendants' counterclaim fails to state any claim upon which relief can be granted for the reasons stated above. The plaintiffs' motion to dismiss the counterclaim will be granted. An appropriate order will issue.

NOTES

1/   The defendants have forwarded as one ground for summary judgment in their favor the contention that the plaintiffs have failed to establish ownership of the copyrights involved in this lawsuit.   The plaintiffs have submitted as exhibits photocopies of a great number of copyright registration certificates.   Registration certificates constitute prima facie evidence of the validity of the copyright and of the facts stated in the certificate. 17 U.S.C. 410(c). We find there is sufficient evidence of ownership by the plaintiffs of certain of the copyrights involved here to allow the Court to determine the issue of whether the defendants' activities constitute copyright infringement.

2/   The named defendants are Redd Horne, Inc., 2823 Corporation, and Glenn W. Zeny individually and doing business as Maxwell's Video Showcase and Maxwell's Video Showcase East.   There is a suggestion in the record that a proper defendant to this action is a corporation known as Maxwell's Video Showcase Limited (MVSL) which has as its sole stockholder Robert W. Zeny. 2923 Corporation has become MVSL as a result of a change in the corporate name.   MVSL operates Maxwell's Video Showcase and Maxwell's Video Showcase East.   Redd Horne, Inc. and Glenn W. Zeny have denied the plaintiffs' allegations of their connection with the alleged infringing activities throughout the course of these proceedings.

3/ It is important to note here what is not at issue in this infringement action. The plaintiffs do not challenge either the possession of the video cassette copies by the defendants or the rental of the cassettes for private in-home use by Maxwell's patrons.

4/ There is only one copy of each film available at each of the two locations at any given time, therefore, if two strangers wish to view the same video cassette at the same time in the store one will be unable to do so.

5/ The in-store rental fee schedule at both Maxwell's locations from noon to 6 p.m. is $5 for two viewers, $6 for three and $7 for four. The cost increases by $1 for each group size from 6 p.m. to closing. Maxwell's charges $2 for a twenty-four hour outside rental and $4.95 for forty-eight hours.

IN THE UNITED STATES DISTRICT COURT

FOR THE WESTERN DISTRICT OF PENNSYLVANIA

COLUMBIA PICTURES INDUSTRIES, INC., EMBASSY PICTURES, PARAMOUNT PICTURES CORPORATION, TWENTIETH CENTURY-FOX FILM CORPORATION, UNIVERSAL CITY STUDIOS, INC., AND WARNER BROS. INC.,
 	
       Plaintiffs
 	
       v.
 	
 REDD HORNE INC., 2823 CORPORATION, GLENN W. ZENY, Individually and d/b/a/ MAXWELL'S VIDEO SHOWCASE, AND MAXWELL'S VIDEO SHOWCASE EAST,
 	
       Defendants
	Civil Action No 83-0016 Erie

O R D E R

AND NOW, this 28th day of Duly, 1983, after hearing, Plaintiffs' Motion to Dismiss Defendants' Counterclaim is GRANTED. Plaintiffs' Motion for Summary Judgment is GRANTED and Defendants' Motion for Summary Judgment is DENIED, and

IT IS ORDERED that

(1)   defendants' counterclaim is dismissed;

(2)   judgment is entered in favor of the plaintiffs and against the defendants;

(3)   upon the posting of a bond in the amount of $50,000, with sufficient surety, an injunction shall issue enjoining the named defendants, their agents, servants, employees and all persons, firms and corporations acting by, with, through or under their authority, direction and control, from performing video cassettes of copyrighted motion pictures owned by plaintiffs at Maxwell's Video Showcase and Maxwell's Video Showcase East in Erie, Pennsylvania, or at any other place open to the public and from performing video cassette copies of copyrighted motion picture owned by the plaintiffs, and

(4) a hearing shall be held at 2:30 P.M. on Thursday September 15, 1983 at the United States Courthouse, Erie, Pennsylvania to afford the parties, pursuant to Sections 504 and 505 of Title 17 of the United States Code, to present evidence relative to the matters of damages, costs, expenses and attorneys fees.

          _____(Glenn E. Mencer)_____
          United States District Judge

cc: counsel of record

Table of Cases

Index

ABOUT THE AUTHOR

Jerome K. Miller attended public and paro- chial schools in Dodge City, Kansas. He holds a bachelor's degree in history (Emporia State), mas- ter's degrees in library science (Michigan) and history (Kansas), and a doctorate in educational media (Colorado). He was a librarian and media specialist at Central Washington State College (now Central Washington University), then taught at the University of Illinois, Graduate School of Library and Information Science. He is now self- employed as an author, speaker, and consultant.

His research and writing concentrate on the application of the copyright law to schools, col- leges, and libraries. His books include: Apply- ing the New Copyright Law: A Guide For Educators and Librarians (American Library Association., 1979) and U.S. Copyright Documents: An Annotated Collection for Use by Educators and Librarians (Libraries Unlimited, 1980). His articles on copyright have appeared in many professional and scholarly journals and two European encyclopedias.

NOTES